MW01173194

Jefferson Avenue Poems

Detroit Days. Twenty-something nights.

A collection of early poetic works

by

Amy L. Alley

"I saw the best minds of my generation destroyed by madness…"

— *Allen Ginsberg*

To the Beat Generation,

who gave me the courage

to find my words,

and the Detroit-area SLAM poets of the

late 90s and early 2000s, who

gave me the courage to

not only find,

but also use,

my voice.

You're all here

in these pages.

Featured Poems

(in order but a totally random order)

Jamaican Blue Mountain Coffee

Tree Hugger

Jefferson Avenue

Blank Canvas (artist's lament)

The Goodbye Poem

Southern Town

Brocey

Beautiful Garden

The Arms of My Oppressor

Beautiful Children

Superman

The Bell

Blink

Jamaican Blue Mountain Coffee

You're having

Jamaican Blue Mountain Coffee

in a cream-colored cup

at a table on a patio

on a street

where we once walked

together.

It's my favorite drink, not yours.

You could barely stand the smell

which you describe as day old dung

being toasted on a grill.

Such a poet.

You don't like it now

any more than you did then

but it's the only thing

you can hold in your hands

that reminds you of me.

Me.

The girl who loved

Jamaican Blue Mountain Coffee

along with other things

like the sound of African drums

played at a street festival

in Ann Arbor.

The conch shell found

at the flea market.

The brass bracelet from Tibet.

Watching birds in the backyard

and the word, *namaste*.

Me.

The girl who knew

who Allen Ginsberg was

and what Frida Kahlo meant

when she said

"I painted my own reality."

Who knew the best day to hit

the resale shops

and what type of lampshade would match

your leopard spot pillow

but wouldn't clash

with the tie-dyed curtains

that should have come down long ago.

Who didn't mind

that you always drank too much

on Fridays

or that you wore T-shirts

with images of bands

that broke up twenty years ago

and in front of her friends

said her coffee smelled

like day old dung.

Funny the things

that people remember about us

when we're not around anymore.

You sit

sipping Jamaican Blue Mountain Coffee

wondering what I thought

was so great about it

while in another world

I sit

and taste the bitter dregs

of a Corona beer

with a lime of course

because that's the way you drank it

and the bitterness takes me back

to you.

You.

Who hated the smell of

Jamaican Blue Mountain Coffee

but loved to smell Hazelnut

which always made me sick.

You.

Who took me to the coffee shop

even though you hated coffee.

Who liked the second-hand record store

downtown

better than the one in the mall

because the people who worked there

were nicer.

Who liked Van Gogh

but didn't get Picasso.

Who liked the necklace I made you

when I didn't have money for a gift

and liked reading magazines

about guitars

in the backseat

on long road trips.

You.

Who liked to quote movie lines

as though they were your own

pearls of wisdom.

Who surprised me at work

with flowers you picked yourself

and again

when you held my hand secretly

under the table

so no one would see

in a crowded bar

in another country

where no one cared anyway.

You.

Who held my hand so tight

that I let go.

Beer goes to my head quick,

and I sleep alone

in a dreamless state.

Coffee keeps you awake

and you sit alone in your room

thumbing through old guitar magazines.

Tree Hugger

"What ever happened to trees?"
You ask what I mean
and I say, *"Look!*
Our nation's most renewable resource
is taking it's time."

You roll your eyes
but I'm serious. I ask you
where you think the wood comes from
to make all the furniture
and decorative bullshit
that is mass produced and
thrust in our faces
for $1.99 at every turn and you say
you don't know or care. I ask you
does it make sense that no one
really questions

where all the wood
from the rainforests
goes
and that no one makes the connection?
You tell me to get real. To quit being
a drag. You turn up the radio.
So I try.
And we ride on, you wondering
why I care about trees and
rainforests anyway
and me wondering why you can't
see the connections.

Years from now, when someone asks you
what happened between us
you'll say that you don't really know,
you just remember
I had issues
with trees.

Jefferson Avenue

'Round the corner you came
chasing me
as I ran down Jefferson Avenue,
laughing.

I didn't stop at the crosswalk
despite the flashing red hand
and the steady hum of traffic. What
the hell
did it matter anyway? And I ran
and you ran
past the deli and the antique shops
downtown
on Jefferson Avenue.

When I closed my eyes
you caught me. Tackled

me from behind,
both of us falling to the ground. One
quick turn, one
fluid gesture
and I made sure you landed first,
hard on that cold concrete.
And I
landed on
you.

You,
Stunned,
scraped,
bleeding,
swearing as you rose,
because I was freed in the fall
and ran ahead, again.
Ran crying now
and the traffic light said stop

but I would not have cared
if it had said die.

I did stop once,
turned around
across the street now
but still
on Jefferson Avenue. I saw you
there, on the corner
seeing me
but too afraid
to cross against the light. Too afraid
of that flashing red hand
too afraid
to run into the blaring roar
of horns and brakes as I had.
You could have caught me
if you hadn't been
afraid. You always were

a better runner. But you waited
until it was safe
and I was gone.

Long off Jefferson Avenue
in no particular hurry, now,
I walk through alleys
passageways
corridors. Past people
and things
that I should fear. This new place,
this strange new place. But
instead of fear
I find the laughter lost
somewhere on Jefferson Avenue.

I walk alone now
amongst this madness
free in this unfamiliar

only because you

were too afraid

to cross

against

the

light.

Blank Canvas
(artist's lament)

Inside my house I'm dreaming

painting

dancing

pictures from my mind

onto that blank canvas.

You look upon me

upon them

in wonder. Think it strange.

But look through my eyes

into my mind. See what lies there.

Come inside.

See how life can be

like a blank canvas. A blank life —

isn't that awful? I won't live that.

Won't be that.

Can't.

Inside my mind
pictures grow and form
like children in their mother's womb.
In my mind
what I experience
takes shape in color
texture
vision. Eyes
upon the canvas. Looking
out. In. Back.
Looks real
to me. Are they real to you?
Real to me
because they are me. Extensions
of me. Look
into my canvas and you
look into me. Can't take it? Others
couldn't, preferred painted lies
and trifles. Realism.

They crave realism, gleaming
perfect harmony. Painted renditions
of the familiar. *"Wow,
it looks so real!"*

II
Artist friends bemoan their servitude
to the cruelest of talents.
Beleaguered minds
and hearts
seek each other out
for comfort because
no one else can understand –
not really –
unless they too can look
at a blank canvas
and see themselves there. Feel
that sudden rush, undulating
desire, lust for color

vision

a vision. Who's vision?

Only the artist's vision

and it's never quite right. What's

in my mind still haunts me,

up at night

wondering why

I just can't seem to get

it right. Other's eyes

fall across my canvas

register shock

distaste or

adoration.

Doesn't matter what I see

behind their eyes

deep down inside I know

it isn't right. Will never

be right. The agony

of needing to do more,

just a bit more, right there. Do
it again, this time,
right.

III
Trapped in me the vision dances out
onto the canvas
in a midnight whirl of energy.
Next morning
I don't recognize it
from the night before. *Did I*
do that? Hey,
did I
do that?
Yes, you did that.
Fear of waking, fear of
rising, fear of letting my eyes fall
upon my own work. My
life's work. Who could understand

such work? Such a need
to put down visions
onto a blank canvas.
Narcissistic tendencies.
Dedicating my whole life to
my own visions. My own passion. This
narcissism, how unpleasant, always in
another world.
Always thinking.
Always dreaming.
"You're always in your head,"
a lover laments before leaving.

IV
"What will you do
with your life, girl?" elders
ask. *"Can't support yourself*
just painting pictures." They say
these words then smile at

exhibitions, sigh, *"I wish*
I had your talent."
I laugh and think of them
choosing sleepless nights
and unpaid bills,
driving home early
from the party, speeding
home to that blank canvas. Gotta
show it who's boss.

V

Talent.
I don't know what that is.
Don't think
I have it, really. I cry in museums
In front of great paintings I
won't do. I cry
with friends whose work doesn't sell
and drink with friends whose does.

I let

my own work go

with trepidation. Reluctance. (It's an

artist thing.)

Fear.

Biting my lip

as they walk away with my baby,

my creation. Do they realize

without me,

without my vision

this paint and canvas would not

have come together

in this way. Do they know

the story, all the stories

that led up to that one painting. What

I had to go through, feel.

What went from me

into that painting, onto that

blank canvas. Or do they merely

think it's pretty? Do they just want
to help me out?

VI
People dabble
in my passion, win awards
with perfect plasticized renditions
that look *so real*, that
treasured word byte,
while my work screams out beside it.
"Little too controversial, girl,"
the powers that be
(*why are there always powers that be?*)
say. *"Think about doing
some wildlife scenes, maybe
paint some flowers."*
Or
*"You paint beautifully, but
your subject matter is just…"*

I stand beside myself because
it's what my painting is.
My visionself.
I celebrate my vision
and myself
while at the same time
wonder why I was given
both a blessing and a curse.
Wonder why I live
beholden to
a blank canvas.

VII
Not a day without
a line, who said that?
Don't remember. But
it haunts me. Makes me turn off the tv
just when the show gets interesting
because I need to work. Haven't

been in the studio all day. Leave
the dinner party early because
I need to work. Haven't
been in the studio all day. Pull away
from his embrace because
I need to work. Haven't
been in the studio all day.
If I didn't
heed the call, would it matter?
Stacks of papers

paintings

canvases
overflow my studio floor. And yet
there's more? More I need to say?
Hours spent at day jobs.
Cost of living
higher each year.
Cost of passion
infinite. What cost? *"Sorry,*

I can't make it tonight.
I need to paint."
They don't understand
the need to paint. The stare of the
blank canvas
back at me.

VIII
Maybe when I'm gone
someone will decide to make me
immortal. Put my work
in museums. Scour through my
journals and letters.
Talk about my genius, my vision.
Talk about me over coffee
in dimly lit cafes in cities where
I've never been. They'll find
my oldest canvases
and ponder them. Even a

doodled signature

on the back of a check

will have value, maybe more

if I die young and tragically.

My family

friends

lovers

might find themselves

subjects of interest

as their faces stare back

from canvases that were

once blank. Staring back at

future generations,

now they too are made immortal

just because they were once

loved by me.

Nah...

that's just my narcissism speaking.
But then
you never know. Did Van Gogh's postman
expect to be famous one day?
What about
the Mona Lisa? Did Wyeth's Christina
expect a deep analysis one day
of her world?

IX
Go on.
I dare you
Be me.
Cut yourself
wide open.
Bleed
onto
a blank canvas.
Run out

into the street

naked.

Expose

to the world

all

that is inside of you. And wonder

if they understand what they see,

if they can ever

understand what you have to endure

to create. If they can ever understand

the painting they say

is a bit '*too much.*'

The one the juried show

did not accept.

The one that evokes tears

from other artists,

because they get it. The one

with a thousand faces,

the one you used

your hands to paint part of
while the sun rose
on another day.

No.
They can't. Their lives
are like blank canvases.
Unpainted, unpossessed by
color
texture
vision
passion.
And you can't be that. Won't
be that. So a million times
a million paintings,
a million times cutting yourself
wide open moments
pass standing, so exposed,
before them, but

they never even notice
you are there. Don't see
your spilt blood
your spilt self
because they prefer
painted lies and trifles.
Realism. They crave safe, gleaming
perfect harmony. Painted renditions of
the familiar. *"Wow, it looks*
so real!

X

The Goodbye Poem

You reach out
stroke my face
smiling
tell me I'm still beautiful to you
that I'll find someone else
that you just want me to be
happy, really.

Lying bastard
you don't care. Deep down inside
you don't care. You just want
off the hook
and you're wondering if you'll
get done with this
in time to get home
and watch *FRIENDS*.

I play along, old pro with you
by now. I just want
you to be happy, too. Smile.
Of course we'll still be friends. Why
shouldn't we be? After all,
you have my best interests at heart.
That's the kind of guy you are.

My broken heart? Pay it no mind.
I'll get over it in time. I smile
across the table
as you nervously fold your napkin
for the tenth time. You smile,
wanting off the hook.

Bastard.
What I really want
is not for you to be happy
but for you to feel one tenth

of the ache welled up inside of me
one tenth
of the sinking feeling that
engulfed me
when you said,
"*We need to talk.*"

I want you to take your hand
and reach inside your chest
and rip your own heart out.
Then stand there,
holding it, blood oozing
between your fingers,
feeling the life drain out of you,
feeling the pain of love ripped away.
Feeling the pain.
Just feeling
something.
Anything

close to what I feel
right now.

Smiling
you kiss me goodbye
on the cheek, 'cause
we're just friends now.
As you walk to your car, leaving me
at the table,
I envision it exploding. Pieces of it,
pieces of you, flying,
falling down all around me
as I finish my dinner.

Ha!

I feel bad about the thought
as you drive away. But only
for a moment. Then, I take

a deep breath
and finish my dinner,
wondering how I'll respond to you
next time
you call.

Southern Town

Southern town

backyard of nowhere

what can you offer

your prodigal daughter?

Returned once more

dusting Northern cities off her jacket

standing here, before you.

World spins 'round in her mind

centrifuge of lights

and nights

and bright-eyed boys. But you,

you are so stable

never changing

Southern town.

II

Confederate monument on Main Street

lies within iron gates

guarded by geraniums

and daughters of a confederacy

long dead. Shows homage

to long-forgotten – what? What

was it, even?

Forgotten by this modern generation

long dead. But you, you still

remember all your ghosts.

Tracing their dead fingers

through cold dates

on your monumental surface

where does the glory lie

that they should be so honored

just for living

and dying

for you,

Southern town.

III

Whistles blow

tired textile workers slumber onward

lines creasing their faces

like the threads

they ply each day. Each day

they are grateful

for that whistle when so many others

have gone silent. Silence

lines the streets of towns

just like you,

where whistles once called out

before moving on to foreign places

(in the name of *cost efficiency* and

other business terms.)

The workers gather

in restaurants with names

like Lucy's Café or Chunky's Place

and order the daily special

consisting of two meats

one vegetable and

sweet tea. Sweet. They laugh

at my vegetarianism

and tell me they love animals

especially

with ketchup.

They also love you,

Southern town. You wear antique shops

and old magnolias like a mantel.

Through

your quiet and stolid streets

I walk, your prodigal daughter,

home again. Home?

I walk alone and wonder at

how you once fit

like a favorite pair of shoes

worn into a perfect state of comfort

kept for many years

until I realized

you were too small for me,

confining even, and just a little

out of style. I traded you in

for something more hip. Still,

sentimental staring

at mammoth white houses

with peeling paint and far too many

rooms...

Stare at them long enough

and they'll stare back at you.

Speak to you, even

but in an older language, one

too hard to understand now. Or maybe

it's just that too few

care to listen.

IV

Children growing up

running barefoot in clover, *"Ma'am"*

and *"Ya'll"* dripping from thier

honeysuckled lips. Growing up

too fast,

former friends pass each other on

grocery aisles

married right out of high school

and now old

at thirty-four, they talk

of work and kids but never mention

dreams. Dreams

die when uttered, here. Better

to sweep them

under your shadows, Southern town.

Watch you loom above them,

regal, and remember. Look

into the eyes of their children

and hope the whistles

are still blowing

when it's their time to work.

V

Southern town

your people love you, still.

The living and the living dead

get excited over

festivals and weddings and

elections. Faces

reflect happiness in store windows

as they pass by. I walk, listening

to rattling trucks,

country boys heading home

to country girls. Would it be easier

if you did fit me? I remember how

they laughed at me up north

because of you.

Just your name

evoked giggles

from too hip people sipping Chardonnay

in glitzy party corners asking me

to say it

one more time, please, because

it sounds

sooooo cuuuuuute.

In smoky Merlot corners

on a million other nights

I defected from conversations

about your politics.

Sooooo cuuuuuuute.

VI

Southern town

like your queen magnolias

all roots go deep, here.

Your daughter,

far from home (*home?*)

looked up from rooftops

into a night sky

where stars were blocked

by clouds of smog

and cicadas didn't sing. Where car

horns and sirens

were the chorus of the night.

A momentary escape

from all the sipping smoking laughing

alone on rooftops

she felt simple

for the first time in her life.

Too many questions asked

about things that happened, times

before hers. Too many questions asked

about you

and your

simplicity,

Southern town.

There must be something here

something you can offer

some retribution. I

defended you, you know. I had to.

Not your politics and stupid monuments

but your queen magnolias

and star-filled cicada nights. Your

simplicity and the way you

curve around

the ones you fit, holding them

so tightly

that they never leave. Can't you

make a little

noise for me now, stir a little

controversy? I wonder

what your old guard would do

if I decided to live my life here

in broad daylight,

to do those kinds of things in this

place where people

just don't do those kinds of things

or rather do but whisper about it

instead of talk. Why must you hold

the long-dead past

in a vise grip

around the future? Why can't you

tuck it away

in a dusty book somewhere

and start new chapters?

VII

Southern town,

men in baseball caps

and women with tired eyes

ask your prodigal daughter

about snow and ice

and how the other halves live. Ask her

how thrilled she is to be home now,

to you

Southern town. And she won't lie.

Instead she turns away, trying hard

to phrase and answer

that will be honest not offensive

to their kind hearts. There is

so much kindness here, really,

though behind her back they whisper

about how much she's changed. The girl

they knew before

is not the same. And they are right.

She's changed. But you haven't,

Southern town. You never do.

And that's

a good thing when the world

outside of you

is spinning. Spinning into

different worlds.

Worlds that will take away your

next generations

because the whistle's days

are numbered

and you know it, Southern town.

But even though

they leave, they will return

from time to time, sitting at

family tables

in front of holiday meals

trying to be who and what they were

before they left you

to find themselves.

They settle into armchairs

after dinner,

trying to sink back into you again

but finding it difficult

to get comfortable. Favorite

pair of shoes

walked all over you

and then away. You are getting

so worn out,

Southern town.

VIII

I will leave you again

and find myself out there

because I can't find me here. The me

I left behind when I walked away from

lemonade on verandas

white shoes and polka dot

Easter dresses

fish frys and dirt tracks

biscuit and cornbread

friends

family

memories of the long dead

etched in stone like you

are etched in me. Though I leave you

you will never leave me,

Southern town. You don't like

to let go

of anything. You are tenacious,

revealing yourself at odd moments

in Ann Arbor bookstores

Toronto Malls

Alaska coffee houses

Phoenix, Arizona

and Seattle

even Cleveland

Minneapolis

Cincinnati

Smoky Windsor lounges

sipping and laughing,

wherever I am, you are too.

You hide yourself so cleverly

only slipping out

when I speak

- *sooooo cuuuuuuuute* -

I speak and they hear you. Smiling.

They can't stand it. Have to ask,

"Where are you from?"

And their eyes dance and twinkle

like the fat robotic Santa in your

Main Street drugstore window

every Christmas since the dawn of time

as I slowly speak your name,

Southern town.

Brocey

Brocey sits
at the foot of my bed
and waits for the silver sliver of sun
that streams through the curtain
each day
about this time. As it eases
its way through
and falls across his marbled body
he looks up.
orange eyes shining
and stares just for a moment
as its warm glow engulfs him
and bathes him
to sleep.

Ah! For the pleasures
in my own life

to be so simple.

Can't believe

I'm envying

a cat.

Beautiful Garden

Step inside my beautiful garden. Look!
See the peonies first, how tall
they are this year. They always
remind me
of you, shy boy, stealing me a
bouquet once
from your mother's garden.

Now see the lilac bush, not yet
in bloom. But trying, silently
working on the greatness that is to
come. I will awake
to an explosion of color one day.
Until then, see the dark leaves.
How quiet they seem,
sleeping there.

Walk over to the irises. One of your
favorites, right?
Van Gogh's too. Many men won't admit
they love flowers,
ah, but you were always different,
never hesitating
to stop and admire a beautiful garden
the way some men admire a
beautiful woman. Breathing in
the sweet perfume, filling your eyes
with color, reaching out to touch
a tender petal just because
you had to feel it. Soft like velvet
between your fingertips,
you would engage
all your senses, almost,
before turning away.

Now see my roses

scarlet once, but they faded fast.
We planted these
together, so careful with
the roots. We were so careful!
And they grew to be lovely. I built
the rest of the garden
around that beauty. Small patches
here and there to accent,
but never equal,
the centerpiece.

I built a lot around those roses
never dreaming that one day
they wouldn't be here.
It happens though.
The things we nurse and tend and love
sometimes die anyway.
I remember those roses.
I carry scars from their thorns.

Remembrances of slow, jagged piercings
scarlet drops of pain, daggers beneath
layers of softness. Scarlet on
scarlet. Wounding me
when I was careless. Just like you.

You, too, were once the centerpiece
I built something beautiful around.
I carry
those scars as well
down beneath the surface.
Ragged jagged edges
daggers ripping through
to where the roots run deep. The roots
we were so careful with,
where the most delicate
of nurturing
once took place.

But that was long ago. It's
spring again now.
I tend my beautiful garden still.
Alone,
I rip from the ground those roots
and pat down the soil with my
bare hands. I rise
among the ruins
and wonder
what I will plant now
in that bare, brown patch
that everything surrounds. That patch
where roots were so strong, once,
and so carefully tended. I wonder how
the roses that once stood
so proudly in the midday sun
have disappeared forever,
leaving nothing but scarlet memories.

Nothing
in the middle
of my beautiful garden
now but
me.

The Arms of my Oppressor

I wake up
breathless
panicked
having nearly succumbed to the
rising damp
that surrounds me like a cold embrace,
unwelcomed.

I peer out the window
at the moon. Ever
watchful sentinel. Silence
becomes one with darkness
and I remember.

I remember eloquence in heartache
and dignity in suffering.
I remember feelings suppressed

thoughts unuttered

(regret! regret!)

and a love to powerful to fall

into patterns

of articulate speech.

I remember words as strong as blows

and a longing that defied

time

distance

and the embrace

of others.

I remember falling

falling

falling

back

and rising up until

once more

I rose as me.

And the moon
ever watchful sentinel
rose too, many times. And many times
darkness became one with silence
and many times I woke up
breathless
panicked
having nearly succumbed to the
rising damp.

And now
I find myself enveloped
in a cloud of calm and conscious
not alone and yet
alone. And once more
falling
falling

falling

back

into the arms of my

oppressor.

Beautiful Children

We used to say
we would have beautiful children.
Remember?
Tall like you
with my dark eyes
and your smile. We'd raise them
up to be
ideal. Perfect little versions
of the you and I we always
dreamed of being.
Molds we never seemed to fit into
they'd surely fill.
And all the while
I would talk and you would smile
we'd lie there in your tattered bed
and on the ceiling overhead
plot the lives of each new child

tall like you
with my dark eyes
and your smile.

We'd talk and talk and talk and talk
and lie there in your tattered bed
and dream. Yet instead,
instead of holding babes
we choose other ways
'cause children come with ties
and strings.
Children would have clipped our wings.
So
with nowhere to grow
together, we grew apart
as lovers do.
And I lost sight of what I was to you.
And what you were to me
stayed on the wind

and the children that we never made

were nothing in the end

but tattered pictures on the wall

Not born into love

not born

at all.

Super Man

Did Superman die?

You stand
naked in front of the bathroom mirror
hung low hung over hung out
unkempt unclean unshaven
undulating irises
another night of excess
another night of dying
just a little more
each day
as you tweak
the same
tired
folly.

Drunken driving madness

locked doors and old whores
crusted vomit on floors
haggard faces unrecognizable at all
rumpled bed and crumpled heads
await you down the hall.

Superman dying. What
would that sound like?

Sound of your own thoughts
sends rivets of pain
daggers in your skull –
please make it stop!

You stare at yourself there
thinking how you
mucked your way through
each day since.
You stood and screamed rage

shook your fists at heaven
in the light of dawn, without
you ripped your own heart out
set it afire
and let the glow from that inferno
dim your pain a little.

You popped pills
popped tops
popped corks
to calm the twitches. Crawled up out
of diggers' ditches
all to find
the answers
for your question: *How do bad things
happen to good boys?*
Good boys
are supposed
to grow up and be good men.

Super men. Not
have to deal with
this shit.

You cried private tears
of anguish, so repentant –
I am so sorry,
really…

You cried
but no one saw
because you were Superman
back then. And Superman
does not apologize.

Somewhere
someplace
someone
else

believed in you
once. Believed you were
like Superman.

Down the hall the woman
in your bed coughs
in her sleep. You don't love her.
She will never
know that moments of sobriety
find you rummaging
through drawers and boxes,
years of paper and accumulated
bitterness, searching for
written ramblings
small worthless treasures -
a phone number written on a
candy bar wrapper,
I love you, faded, written on a napkin
slipped to you across the

table one night
in another life. Kodak moments,
smiles frozen in time
proof that once upon a time
you wanted to be
thought you could be
were
Superman.

Can't even wash your hands now
for the shaking. Sink clutter
can't find soap or clean towels.
Does it
even matter? Why be clean on
the outside and
wretched underneath?
Your heart and soul and lungs
and brain and
all of it just wretched.

Superman, tell me again,

how many fifths you put away

that night? How many

pills passed over your tongue?

Did you roll them around first

or swallow them all, right away?

Do you remember?

"Hey where you going? What are you doing out there? Get off the ledge before you fall! Have you been drinking again? What's wrong with you? Answer me, what's wrong with you? Are you mad? Are you okay? Get down now, I really mean it, you can't fly! Come on back inside, who do you think you are anyway? Superman? Oh my God! Oh my God! What did he do? Call someone!"

What does it feel like,

finding out that you can't fly?

Toilet flushes you into awareness
Hollow metallic memory

"Is he alive?"

So much pain.
Blood everywhere.
You remember red and yellow
lights, flashing, blinding
but you could see.
You were
alive.
The world
was just different now,
red and yellow
blinding
bathed
in light.

Somewhere

someplace

someone

else

believed in you once

wrote *I love you* on a napkin

and smiled at you

above the red and yellow light

of candles, flickering.

Crumpled bed and bedmate stare at you

as you stand in the doorway

otherwise empty

and watch the play of sunlight spread

across her worn-out smile.

You don't love

her, not this one. You rub

your burning eyes

tired now so tired

and still burning. You wish
you could remember
what the doctor said that shrink
they sent you to
afterwards. What did he say?
"Hell is private"
as if you didn't know, as if
you didn't burn
a little more
each day.

Superman.
Everyone loved him.
Hero in a suit and tie. Superman
never got drunk
and slapped his girl. Never
yelled, never
lost control
never lost

at all.

I love you faded on the napkin now.

Hold it up to the light, yes,

it's still there. Superman never

stayed out all night.

Never lost his job and stayed in bed

all day, only rising to drag himself

out into the blinding

burning

light of day searching for

a drink, a hit,

drug down

into that part of town

doing anything,

almost anything,

to fix the mess

that you became.

It never lasted.

One drink, one swallow
down it goes, bitter, hollow
burning you away
just a little more
each day. For that one moment
to forget
or maybe just forgive
a little. Screaming rage,
shaking your fists at heaven.
A fix.
What did it fix?
You?
You were never broken.
Not really.

Superman.
Do you remember
little boy racing home from
school each day

to watch his favorite hero
save the world on cable?

Superman.

Tell me again
as you slide down onto the floor
back against the wall,
too tired to stand.

Super man,
who did you
grow up to be?

The Bell

I remember, as a child
my cousins and I
exploring my neighbors' backyards.
Feral children, we
discovered one day,
to our delight,
in the yard of a house nearby,
a bell.
An old schoolyard bell
on a tall wooden post. Cast iron
dulled by ages, standing tall. A
rusted testament to what was
once a schoolyard
but was now a backyard
where the laughter of children
was long replaced
by the scuttle of leaves

on an asphalt drive.

But we didn't care about that then.
What mattered to us
was the long rope
with the knot on the end
that dangled
just above our heads
but still within reach
of our child arms.

We each had a turn on the rope,
thin arms pulling with all our might
until we heard that one loud
resonance and knew
we had rung the bell. And we laughed
with delight each time
though it always sounded the same.

Then suddenly! A shrill voice!
The owner of the house with the bell
in the backyard was not amused.
Stooped, weathered figure standing
on the back steps
holding a broom like a sword,
screaming a litany
of insults at the motley group of
children who had dared
come onto her property and give sound
to what was silent.
How we ran
- *so fast* -
me, the oldest,
leading the charge.
Out of control and crying,
no comprehension
of the wrong we did, words
police, jail, and *brats*

ringing in our ears, her cold eyes
in our memory.

We were never going back.

But...

A few days later we mustered up
our courage
and returned, only to find the
long rope
severed crudely, the remains dangling
out of reach of our child arms.
The bell forever
silent.

Now I am grown,
the broom wielding homeowner
long dead,

and the bell in the backyard of
the house nearby is gone.
Who knows where?
Replaced
by a modern playset where children
now swing and climb and play all day
in this yard
that once was a school yard.
I think something
has been restored here. This place
is happy now. And I wonder
if she knows,
that broom wielding homeowner,
who preferred the silence
of the bell
to the laughter
of children.

Blink

Do you see me?

Blink.
Did that help? I am
here, you know...
Don't think that I don't know
you see me
hear me
feel me...
but you go on.
Pretend I am invisible.
Go on.

Blink. Blink.
Do you see me now?
Everyone else seems to just fine.
Only you refrain.

Only you
make me seem invisible
so casually,
as if it doesn't matter. Well go on.
Pretend I am
invisible.
Go on.

Blink. Blink. Blink.
Do you see me here, beside you?
When you were lost, you seemed to.
You seemed to see me everywhere,
remember? I do.
You can make me seem invisible
You can make me be invisible
to you
but you can never make me
not remember. I remember
everything

quite clearly. So go on.
Pretend I am
invisible.
Go on.

Blink. Blink. Blink. Blink.
Do you see what I remember?
Do you know what it is
that I recall?
I think you do.
I think that you pretend you
do not see me
because you remember, too.
Now. But for a long time
you didn't. Then one day
you saw me again.
And it all came back.
You don't want it back.
So you tell yourself

that you don't see me. Tell yourself
I am not there. You like the new self
that you carved out
and lived out
and can live out
because no one else knows.
No else remembers. No one
but me. So you go on.
Pretend I am
invisible.
Go on.

Blink. Blink. Blink. Blink. Blink.
That's right. I'm still here.
Because we both know quite well
I am not invisible. Your secret
calling to me
says as much. Sitting alone,
inside yourself,

wondering just how much

I remember

until you can't stand it anymore

and have to ask. I don't reply.

You can't move on.

Hung up in the you that was,

you must have some kind of hold on me

to release yourself.

So you decide

I am invisible

and cease to see me.

In crowds you cease to see me

though everyone else can. In thought

you cease to hear me though

I drown out

everything else in your mind.

In dreams

you cease to feel me though I am there

beside you in your bed. But you go on.

Pretend I am
invisible.
Go on.

Blink. Blink. Blink. Blink. Blink.
Blink.
Blink become a tic
and you frighten people
whenever I am near
because they can plainly see me,
why can't you? You babble on
incessantly
about the new great things you've done
and things you've yet to do
until the babble in your head
becomes the dialogue that you look
forward to most
at the end of each day. You grit
your teeth hard
and tell yourself I am not real

therefore, you cannot hear me

when I speak.

But you still do. You hear

what I don't say above

everything else.

It's deafening.

So go on.

Pretend I am

invisible.

Go on.

Blink. Blink. Blink. Blink. Blink.
Blink. Blink.

Blink back the tears

that fall when you remember

everything that you forgot. Worked

so hard to forget. I feel

a little sorry

that you can't escape you now.

I escaped you

long ago.

Tic becomes a twitch.

Now and then you catch a whiff,

a smell like dime-store perfume

you remember buying

but that I never wore. And you

tell yourself

it isn't real, because it isn't.

When we meet by accident

you look away, which

you wouldn't need to do

if I weren't really there. So go on.

Pretend I am

invisible.

Go on.

Blink. Blink. Blink. Blink. Blink.
Blink. Blink. Blink.

You lie awake at night

because you refuse to dream again.

Refuse

to succumb to a state

where you can't be in

control. Subconscious knows

that I am real. Knows I am here.

Insomnia takes away the dreams

the dreams where I am not invisible

but real and you can

see me

hear me

feel me.

So you no longer sleep. You lie

in an empty state

in an empty bed

in an empty house

of your own choosing.

And in the morning

when you rise I am not there.

You are relieved

so relieved
you sit and cry
for the lost dreams. But go on.
Pretend I am
invisible.
Go on.

Blink. Blink. Blink. Blink. Blink.
Blink. Blink. Blink. Blink.
You try and you try and you try
and you become mad with trying
to make me invisible. When
others speak to me
you writhe inside. When
others touch me
you want to die. But it's too
late now. Too late
to go back and undo all those memories
all those wasted hours
dreamless nights.

You decide you want to

see me

hear me

feel me

even if it means facing down

that old you

once again, once and for all.

You decide that I am real now

and that in me lies

every dream you cast aside.

You decided one sleepless night

that if I have forgiven you

then maybe you can forgive you, too

and that maybe seeing me again

won't be so bad. So you go on.

But now I am

invisible.

Go on.

BlinkBlinkBlinkBlinkBlink
BlinkBlinkBlinkBlinkBlink
Fast.
You try to find me again
but people shake their heads
and tell you I am not there
when you know you just saw me.
When you hear me
and respond, people move away
because no one else is there.
You feel nothing.
Deep in sleep you dream nothing.
And you see nothing
in front of you
where I once was. Waiting,
waiting so long,
for you to see me. You reach out
in your mind
across a sea of recollection

and still I am not there.

You blink and tic and twitch

yourself into a frenzy

and you scream out to anyone

and everyone,

"Why can't she

see me

hear me

feel me

anymore?"

You sit alone in a world of

your own making,

breaking.

Others come and go and pass you by

and you blink

and blink

and blink

and blink

and blink

and blink

and blink

and blink

and blink

and blink

and blink

and blink

and blink

and blink

and blink

and blink

but

it doesn't even matter

because when you hold your hand

up to your eyes

there's nothing there, just the

memory of what

your hand should look like.

You aren't there.

You are invisible.

You sit amongst the passers by

and cry out to them

but they can't

see you

hear you

feel you.

You aren't there.

You turn around

in time to catch a glimpse of yourself

fading into nothing.

And you know, now,

the sweet, sharp,

stinging pain

of being made

invisible.

Go on.

The poems in this collection reflect
the time I spent, in my mid-to-late
twenties, living in the Detroit area.
Slam poetry was the big scene. I had

discovered the work of the Beat poets
and was finding my voice as an artist
as well as a poet. Many, if not most,
of these poems were written to be
performed on stage. But I hope you
enjoy reading them instead. There is
nothing like the poetry of one's youth
to remind the self how far we come
from where we start. So many poets and
friends from my Detroit days
influenced these works, influenced my
life, inspired and lifted me up in so
many ways. There are friends I still
see and speak to today, but there are
also friends lost to time, whose last
names I can't remember and poets I can
still see performing on stage but
whose true names I never knew. I wish
I did. I'd like to reach out to them
now and say thank you, thank you for
authentically being you at a time when
I was authentically learning to be me.
This book is dedicated to you all.

Shine on!

"What I Learned There"

Amy L. Alley

Made in the USA
Columbia, SC
21 March 2023

13925375R00071